Fashioned by the Master Designer

I've loved fashion ever since I was a young girl. There was a show I loved to watch with my daughter called "What not to Wear" which premiered on TLC network and lasted for ten years. Two people collaborated to give their perspective on what people should and should not wear. In that vein, it's time for your own personal makeover – from God's perspective!

1. Don't wear blame – God wiped your slate clean, don't keep dishing out the blame and shame game. Yes, you've been hurt; yes, you were treated unfairly; yes, you have been abused and so many more ugly attacks were thrust upon you. BUT take hold of the grace that God gives you every morning. Don't feel condemned over what you did or what happened to you. Receive EVERYTHING our Daddy has to offer. Don't reject it. It's time to move forward.

2. Don't wear the same thing – oftentimes people go into detail about prayer requests and ask you to pray the same thing over and over again. Pray, believe, wait for your change to come by putting your trust in God and, by faith, SEE IT BEFORE YOU SEE IT! When you are stuck in the same thing year after year you are not changing your mindset nor are you changing your healing wardrobe. You are repeating an outfit that is not in season. It's outdated and expired so please let it rest. You are dressing in the wrong season, falling back when it's time to spring forward to healing and deliverance. You are wearing and reliving the painful wardrobe of 1990 when its 2016. Put on your garment of praise and let the rest go! Let go of the dreadful relationships and the guilt of your past! Your past may have had you stuck but change your wardrobe, change your mindset and spring into your season of embracing the love and everything else God has for you. Love yourself!

3. Don't wear the fame – you were known in the past for being sorrowful, a liar, a hater, insecure...you were famous for this! God has decided that you are chosen! Let go of the fame that you used to be known for. Be remade; you are long overdue for a spiritual makeover. Most times this makeover requires a change in the company you keep. Everyone may not be able to receive the new and improved you. People who don't believe in your God won't believe in your change. Be honored instead of offended that you are no longer invited to where you use to be invited. It's an honor to be set apart. Some people are in your life for a season while others are intended to remain for a lifetime. Some outfits you wear are vintage – you can wear them and they won't ever go out of style so you wear them with class and dignity; but some things in your closet are outdated so spruce it up. Change what you are wearing. Experience some TLC - you deserve it! Be a new and improved you! You are fashioned by God - The Master Designer. He's better than any designer bag or shoe! He dresses you with meekness and salvation. He has bought you with a price, wrapped you in beauty and adorned you with fine linen. So be the princess He created you to be. You are royalty! You are an overcomer! You are FASHIONED BY THE MASTER DESIGNER.

Walking by Faith

The heavens declare the glory of God; the skies proclaim the work of his hands. Day after day they pour forth speech; night after night they reveal knowledge. They have no speech, they use no words; no sound is heard from them. Yet their voice goes out into all the earth, their words to the ends of the world. (Psalm 19:1-4)

As I write this, I am looking out into the beauty of God's artwork! Trees sway effortlessly in the early morning breeze so high up in the mountains. The beautiful bird chirps ever so beautifully from 11 p.m. until 1:30 a.m. when I awakened. The sunrise and sunset are so beautiful to me and the emotional state I am currently in is hard to contain. In many ways the beauty is simply more than anyone can possibly take in and yet we as human beings continue to be deeply drawn to it. Why is this? When we see things in this world that cause us to marvel with amazement we should recognize them as windows through which we see the beauty of God –how wonderful!

Yesterday when I arrived in Costa Rica I was immersed into a glimpse of what my son will be doing in this beautiful country. Captivated by his pure selflessness and marveling at the God in him my chest felt an explosion that was hard to keep hidden! These people love him here! They kissed me and thanked me for "allowing" my son to serve them for a year. Little do they know that my son was born for this! The thing that I am in awe of is that he is doing it while AFRAID! He told me last night that when I leave it's going to be even more real what he is doing. But this is the great commission, which we are ALL called to! I have so much to share but I do not want to tell it all in one letter. Just know that we are living this life not for ourselves but to fulfill our purpose. We can run from the call that is placed on our lives or we can embrace it. It's a choice. Live outside of your selfishness and avail yourselves to others. Yes all of us have daily tests and anguish; however when you begin to serve others God will always take care of your situation. Embrace the beauty of servitude. Relinquish selfishness and walk in purpose! I boarded that plane from comfortable Ohio with a plethora of emotions! I wanted to kiss my son and say go in peace and run back to his dad who stood watching his first true love and first born depart. Yet the spirit in me whispered sweetly "I will hold your hand if you just allow me to" and at that moment I felt protected and safe.

Last night, after settling into this massive and beautiful room, my son knocked on the door. He said mom, I will be fine. I saw so many things in his eyes so I looked up to his 6 foot self, kissed him and told him not to be afraid...."God's got you!" His response was "yes ma'am. I just want you to be ok with this." I said "I am. It's hard but I am."

When he shut the door to my room, I heard his footsteps fade and was reminded of a line in that beautiful poem *Footprints in the Sand*. The last thing I remember saying to God before falling into a peaceful sleep is God how did you send your only begotten son from a comfortable place without shedding a tear! I decided then that I would have no more tears, just peace. God allowed me to have sweet sleep and I am ready to embrace another day here awaiting the next heart throbbing mission.

Emotions...

We ought always to thank God for you, brothers and sisters, and rightly so, because your faith is growing more and more, and the love you have for one another is increasing. (2 Thessalonians 1:3) My faith has increased, my love has increased and my compassion for others – especially those who are different from me – has gone to a level that's hard to even imagine. I believe that emotions are meant to move people towards God. I have cried incessantly in just 24 hours! I've met new sisters in Christ who I will pray for continually. I will support financially and will definitely be praying for the opportunity to come back! A piece of my heart will be left here, not only because I will be leaving my son but also because I will be journeying away from the quick yet meaningful relationships I've formed. I never ever thought I would travel to another country and encounter such big hearted, selfless, loving people.

I started the New Year with savings goals but yesterday I decided to give more by faith! My husband and I have supported missions for many years but I want to give even more now! While we are taking the time to invest money and save for our future it is also time to raise the bar as I prepare to invest more financially & emotionally into people & relationships. Emotional deposits today will bear fruit not only presently but for eternity. Emotional investments today pay the dividends of oneness which illustrates our faith in Christ. Excited to see where my faith will take me!

Stay tuned!

My Prayer: Lord I am in awe of Your sense of humor. You knew that I'd never take this journey in life unless You sent one of my kids abroad! You are so wise and I love the strategic plan You have for my life! Help this introverted, emotionally-charged daughter of Yours stretch even more. May I ask a huge favor though: will You slow down just a tad bit? I need a little rest to digest what I am in the midst of; I'm embracing and, quite frankly, enjoying this season but this is a lot, God! Looking forward to what the days ahead will bring.

Built to last

I am discovering what I am made of and being with the lover of my soul is paradise as He continues to perfect me.

Departing my first born was surreal. His hug was tight. I felt his heart beat rapidly; or was that mine? I spoke words to him that were sacred. I didn't want to let him go but I know he has a mission to accomplish. I told him that I am confident he will be just fine. When I released him I hugged him once again, prayed and spoke life into him, and told him that he was built to last!

God requires more from us than just saying yes to Him. As much as I love my husband, children, family, church & friends the love I have for Jesus is immeasurable. I am able to love better because of the Father. I always say "I love love."

Leaving a Legacy

Do not say four more months and then the harvest, open your eyes and see that the fields are ripe for harvest. (John 4:35)

The legacy we leave is predicated on the people we invest.

Anything worth doing is worth doing well. If you are building a family, frame it well. Furnish it with faith, love, hope, and the fear of God. Pour a foundation of honesty, trust, and excellent work.

If you are building a life, develop it with discipline, forgiveness, humility, grace, service, and obedience to God. Spend your time building relationships, processes, projects, and enterprises that are sustainable and eternal. Seek to focus on endeavors that contribute to and facilitate faith-based initiatives. Indeed, build up people who will improve on your accomplishments. Above all else, dedicate your building to God, carefully constructed with the bricks of vision, mission, and values. They are embedded in the foundation of the enterprise. Strategy, objectives, goals, and metrics all flow from the same source. Where there is vision, there is a compelling cause that motivates everyone. Where there is mission, there is clarity of purpose. Where there are values, there is an agreed-upon behavior that defines the culture.

If your vision is prayerfully aligned with God's will, then He will accomplish great things through you and others. Cast a God-sized vision that will last beyond your lifetime.

Family Heritage

Yesterday I was an emotional wreck! I received news about a procedure my dad was having. Speaking to him via FaceTime brought me a little comfort however I still wanted to see him. I kept thinking "what if I lost my dad" and I begin to sob (although the procedure wasn't life threatening he's 72 so I had some concern). I thought about how much I've always wanted to be a "daddy's girl" and, even though my sister won that spot, I still love him so much. Just a couple of years prior I was barely in communication with him because of hurt and offense but since we've reconciled I've developed a renewed love and respect for him. My family is as dysfunctional as the next but I am blessed to have been given the parents that were picked just for me!

Your family background is part of God's story for your life: the good, the bad and the ugly! Your unique story is penned by God's grace with spattered ink blots of love. The antagonist is the devil, the hero is Jesus and the one being rescued is you. Past guilt and ignorance doesn't need to shame and define you because you have been bought and adopted by Christ. Health and wealth are not your family's security—the eternal security of Jesus is where you find peace and joy. Your family background is a testament to the transforming power of God in your life today.

Jesus came to earth from heaven, so those of us on earth could go to heaven. He was born to a virgin whose family background was as diverse as most of our own. Encouragingly, Christ's genealogy is made up of an array of people including farmers, soldiers, kings, a prostitute and unbelievers. Jesus was sinless but He came from a long line of sinners. His family background is full of those who needed the Lord and others who loved the Lord. He was born in God's timing, in a tiny town, to be the Savior of the world. His family background was part of God's unique story.

"But when the fullness of the time had come, God sent forth His Son, born of a woman, born under the law, to redeem those who were under the law, that we might receive the adoption as sons." (Galatians 4:4-5)

Like my husband emphatically says: "Be who you is and not who you is not! "

Wherever we find ourselves we are not alone. If our earthly family ignores us we have a heavenly family that accepts us. We may be closer to the blood-bought family of Christ than our own blood relatives. Our faith family is forever with Jesus!

Prayer: Heavenly Father, thank You for my family background. Use me to influence my family toward faith in Jesus! Help me to be a light! Help me to walk in forgiveness. Help me to see my flaws and humbly acknowledge them as I draw closer to You. I'm so happy to be called "Your Girl." Allow me to represent You, Daddy, well!

Baggage Claim

I AM CLOTHED WITH STRENGTH AND DIGNITY AND I WILL LAUGH AT DAYS TO COME.
(Proverbs 31:25)

Instead of concentrating on my problems and getting discouraged, I'm choosing to focus on God and meditate on His promises for me. A scary situation turned into a miracle. Boarding the plane to Costa Rica with my son we unfortunately didn't have seats next to each other – he paid for me to have an upgraded seat because he knows his mama is high maintenance. As we were boarding this huge plane I asked him to give me my baggage. In this moment he realized that he'd been distracted by being on the phone talking to his girlfriend when he picked up his baggage he'd inadvertently left mine. He said "mom once we are seated I will go back and get yours." I tried for 2.2 seconds to remain calm but that didn't last long. I broke into a sprint, saying excuse me over a dozen times to the passengers and just about pushing people out of the way because I couldn't relax! My baggage contained my passport, a priceless scripture blanket my best friend had given me years ago which I travel with EVERY where I go and my wallet containing all of my cash. When I made it to the terminal my baggage was sitting right where he left it! I ran back onto the plane, succumbing to incessant hot flashes, moments before departure. As I settled in the stewardess asked "Are you seated in first class?" and I said "Yes," not really processing her question. About a minute after sitting down I realized I was in the wrong seat so I got her attention and apologized for misunderstanding her. I told her that I was seated in the wrong place but she insisted that I wasn't. I showed her my ticket but she countered with "Ma'am this is your seat." She was trying to hurry up and check the overhead compartments and I was obviously distracting her. Once she came back I asked her to look at my ticket and realized I was right but told me not to worry about it. There I was sitting in First Class when my son had only paid for Business Class!

During this amazing First Class experience I began to think, "Shoot I could get used to this!" After much eating and being catered to I began to think about how I got to this place. It took something bad happening for me to "win" a prize I didn't deserve! To think, the reason my son took the baggage from me was because it was heavy. I'd carried it around for a long time but the thought never crossed my mind that he would forget it BUT I'd recover it and experience sweet peace.

There are so many spiritual parallels in this story but, because my mama told me my anecdotes are good but too long, I'm choosing to focus on these bullet points:

1. Let go of your baggage (Ephesians 4:31)
2. Chase after healing, restoration and forgiveness
3. Experience rest through faith
4. Embrace the benefits of releasing the anxiety and surrender to the miraculous blessings God has waiting for you when you LET IT GO!

Prayer: God I struggled this week even after letting go of something valuable last week and seeing how quickly You restored me, in a way that exceeded what I could've imagined. I've suffered blow after blow Monday through Friday and I've cried tears of hurt and anger. Feeling justified with each emotion I found myself so exhausted but You are reminding me this morning that You graced me to endure it until this point. I didn't stop praising You; I didn't quite handle each situation as I probably should have but You covered me with grace and compassion because You are forever building my faith muscles through difficult situations. Thank You for helping me realize that being a giant requires stamina and endurance. I live to make You proud of me. Thanks for offering new grace this morning and forever championing me and sending angels to minister to me when I want to allow the flesh to have full control. God, You are amazing and I'm so thankful for the blessings as well as the trials that will forever come because You give enduring power that will carry me though it all. I'm so in awe of You! I love you Daddy and um...thanks for loving me!

Ready to quit right before the miracle happens

Life is hard. Giving up is easy. Staying and persevering is tough but proven to be worth it. I find myself being motivated and determined to be the best ME. I love on many people but am close to a select few. I'm not the one to talk on the phone daily but my close inner circle knows my heart. What stings more than anything is betrayal. Many years ago I had a very close friend – let's just say we did "life" together – but what hurt so deeply was when clear boundaries were unexpectedly crossed. I have to admit that naiveté was present and with that I was totally caught off guard when the ultimate betrayal transpired. Now we've seen each other from time to time over the many years since this huge devastation but I was determined that I would never get close to anyone outside of my immediate family ever again; I just couldn't imagine investing so much into another relationship. Literally within days of this betrayal God sent another person into my life who pours into me, loves me, supports me, encourages me and challenges me. I didn't want to befriend this person but she was persistent and finally I realized it was a God connection. Betrayal of any kind can affect multiple areas of your life. Ever since this life-changing incident I am slow to relinquish my heart to people. I am extremely close to my mother and sisters but even with that closeness the three of us have a unique bond. I don't talk to them daily but they know that our love goes deep and there is NOTHING I would not do for those three women.

Every single one of us is wired to have personal connections, some on a big scale and some on a smaller, more intimate scale. Vulnerability is the gateway to the intimacy we crave. But it takes serious guts to push the limits of vulnerability, to dig deeper and deeper into the core of who you are and not only love and accept those imperfect parts of yourself, but to expose them to someone else. All the while hoping, trusting and praying that they will be held sacred.

So I finally decided one day to take my grieving heart to the foot of the cross! I had done my share of journaling about the anger and remorse I felt. I felt justified in my pain but I had to be careful that bitterness didn't take root. One day I was reading a recommended book about venomous people and I soon realized that I had to pray for my enemies, give them over to God and release all of those negative emotions I was feeling. It is not easy. I find myself having to take this grieving heart to the cross daily. Not inadvertently hurt people in some cases but I want grace given to me so I must extend it as well. Misunderstandings will occur but how we handle and process them is crucial. The biggest miracle is forgiving and moving forward.

Which will you choose? I choose "love."

Above all, love each other deeply, because love covers over a multitude of sins. (1 Peter 4:8)

Prayer: God give me a heart transplant. I want your heart; I want to see people as you see people. I want to love the way you love, I want to forgive the way you forgive. I can't do this on my own! Help me to love those who are hard to love. God, that is a tough one because I am content with You loving them and me leaving them but I want Your will to be done and not my own. I want to glorify You and make You proud of me. I confess my struggles and embrace Your hand of mercy. I pray for Your guidance every step of the way. I want to be used by You and with this I know that offense will come; hurt will come because You are creating a precious gem that won't crumble under pressure! Use me for Your glory! I am smart enough to know by now that being used and hurt comes with the territory. Help me through the tears, knowing that You will carry and comfort me in the process. Thank you, Daddy, for Your continued love that You pour on me so that I can reflect and represent You as best as I can. I believe but please help me to accomplish this hard task. In Jesus' name I pray and definitely believe. Amen

You are someone else's miracle

Sunday morning my husband and I were heading to church and passed a church sign that read "You are someone else's miracle." I think one of the most important things we can do while we are on this earth is help others. Every day we all have the opportunity to be someone's miracle. I believe that you may not change the entire world, but you can change someone else's world by being their miracle.

What is a miracle? It's thinking beyond you and giving back to the world. It's taking the spotlight off you and shining it on someone else. It's realizing that life is not always about you. I wonder where I would be if wonderful people hadn't helped me when I needed it. What would my life be like if teachers, family, friends, and mentors hadn't helped me? What if no one had reached back to pull me forward? You have to remember that whatever you achieve in life isn't accomplished by yourself. An African proverb says it takes a village to raise a child. In other words, part of who you are comes from the positive influence of those around you. You didn't arrive here by yourself.

How do you give? You can give in ways that you'll remember for the rest of your life or in ways that you might forget next week. What difference can one person possibly make? Yesterday I was on video Skype with my son as I traveled to the Chicago area to check on my "healing" father. I was blessed when he shared with me a text from one of the hosts I stayed within Costa Rica. It read: "Patrice this is Carol. We are in my house celebrating my birthday and your son is with us. He is fine & keep trusting that your Heavenly Father is also his Father. When you say that I remind you of yourself it is an honor I cannot accept. I can't even untie the laces of your shoes but we share something, the love of Christ, which unites us. I hope to see you again and I'm glad you keep us in prayer."

I was humbled that I'd made an impact in her life through one short visit.

You can make a difference! Have you ever noticed that when you focus on someone else's problem, your problems don't seem to be so bad? You can also be someone's miracle. All it takes is the right attitude. Whenever you find someone with a bigger problem than yours, become their miracle. While you are becoming their miracle, they may become yours. The miracle you make could be as simple as listening to someone.

I am a miracle! Are you?

A generous person will prosper; whoever refreshes others will be refreshed. (Proverbs 11:25)

Love You or Leave You

I'm sure each of us can think of someone, either past or present, who we have seen as unlikeable for one reason or another; and if not by us then by others. Maybe it's their personality, habits, demeanor … or maybe they are downright rude and inconsiderate of those around them. It's generally taken for granted in society that there will be people we just don't like or get along with. It's normal—and we shouldn't worry too much about making an effort to befriend them. "If they get on my nerves, isn't it just better to let them be than to risk more annoyance and possibly even greater friction?"

As a Christian, is this the mindset we should have toward those who we deem "unlikeable?" Should we just go with the flow, so to speak, and allow the world to shape our thinking about who we love or don't have to love? Or is our first thought to turn the Word of God to truly know what God's heart is on the matter?

Confession: My experience has been "I can love you or leave you;" if we aren't compatible then goodbye. No love lost, life continues. I see you, speak to you, love you from afar and continue on with life...NEXT. My devotion today has me re-examining my philosophy. Taking it to the cross!

In Luke 10, Jesus is having a conversation with a lawyer and to test Jesus he asks what he should do to inherit eternal life. Jesus then asks the lawyer what he thinks the answer is, to which he replies, *"You shall love the Lord your God with all your heart and with all your soul and with all your strength and with all your mind, and your neighbor as yourself"* (Luke 10:27). Jesus confirms this as the right answer, and to further justify himself the lawyer asks, *"And who is my neighbor?"* In response, Jesus tells the story of the good Samaritan (read Luke 10:30-37). The Jews and Samaritans hated one another, yet Jesus was telling them to love, serve, and give to those who they considered their enemies.

It's not your gift it's HIS gift

A spiritual gift is given to each of us so we can help each other. (1 Corinthians 12:7)

Dear Lord, let me use my gifts and let me help others discover theirs. Your gifts are priceless and eternal. May we use them to the glory of Your kingdom, today and forever. Amen

My grandbaby took my phone from me yesterday and said "Mine" and I said how about ours? She continued to say "Mines" so I took the phone from her and I tried explaining to a 16-month old that Paw Paw gave it to Grandma and Grandma will let you hold it for a minute but let's share. Sometimes as believers we are generously given entrusted gifts from God. How are you using the gift? Are you sharing it with the body of Christ for edification? Are you being selfish with it? Did you know that you can abuse the gift? He gave all of us gifts. The best way we can thank God for these gifts is to use them for His glory.

To demean the gift is to insult the gift giver! He uses leaders to help develop those gifts. Pastors are always challenging their congregations to discover their gifts and to fine tune them. There are times when we can get puffed up with that gift so please be careful! "Well I can preach better than the pastor." "I can hit that note better than she can so I should've led that song." "The kids in children's ministry love for me to teach, I'm their favorite." "My OxTails taste better than hers in hospitality ministry so I should be the designated person to fix that dish at every pot blessing!" Be careful and know that a proud spirit is ugly in the sight of God.

Promise yourself that you will earnestly seek to discover the talents that God has given you. Then nourish those talents and make them grow. Finally, vow to share your gifts with the world for as long as God gives you the power to do so. After all, the best way to say "Thank You" for God's gifts is to use them.

When I discovered my gifts I began to soar with them. I am learning to protect the gifting and anointing on my life and also being careful not to allow people to abuse some of the gifts! Examine the gifts that God has given to you. How are you using them?

Just imagine what the world would be like if we began to steward the gifts God has given us to serve one another, to serve the body of Christ and to be a blessing to those we come in contact with! What a powerful impactful Christians we would be!

No prayer is wasted

Each prayer is duly noted by God and answered at just the right moment.

Spending time alone with God rids our minds of distraction so that we can focus on Him and hear His Word. By abiding in Him we enjoy the intimacy to which He calls us and come to truly know Him. Jesus actually instructed us to pray to God alone at times: "When you pray, go into your room, close the door and pray to your Father, who is unseen" Matthew 6:6.

When we're alone with God, we draw closer to Him and get to know Him in a different way than we do in group settings.

I reminisce often of those early days of raising my children. One that stands out in my mind is when I would have that quality one on one time with each of them. I sometimes allowed them to choose where we would go for our dates. I love holidays, whether they're man-made or "Patrice made." This particular date was a Saturday afternoon in February leading to Valentine's Day. I'd already taken Twin A on a date of his choosing the weekend prior. It was time for Twin B to decide where she wanted to go. So when I asked, her response was no surprise to me; she said "LIBRARY" and I got so tickled! So off to the library we went. I decided to take her to the BIG library downtown Columbus. She lit up like a Christmas tree. We spent an hour there with her walking the aisles finding books and asking how many can she take home. I said as many as your little arms can hold and she hugged me so tight! She picked chapter books and I was so proud of her! Last Sunday I gave her a baby shower and as I helped her put all of the gifts away she sat in the nursery organizing the books, with that same little girl smile on her face and I begin to get emotional. I spent so many years pouring into my children, praying with and for them, trusting God that I would make Him proud with the seeds I've planted in these precious lives He's blessed and entrusted me. To see these prayers manifest in their adult lives is beyond rewarding! During those years of being a stay at home mom I watched friends soar in their careers. I had many down days, feeling insecure and wished I could have chased my dreams but I had many moments such as this testimony that makes me say that it was so worthwhile! None of my prayers were wasted. I believe that my children will pour into their children as I did with them. They will have alone time with their kids and they will build memories and monuments of faith deposits. I prayed specific blessings over my children and it's so amazing seeing them come to life then and now but it was in HIS timing that I would see them manifested. I will never stop praying and spending time with my Daddy! I love the relationship I have with Him. He is my best friend, my Valentine...the lover of my soul.

Intimacy involves some alone time. Close parental relationships are those in which children and parents have special "alone time" together. Spending time alone with a loved one provides the opportunity to truly come to know that person. Spending time alone with God is no different. When we're alone with God, we draw closer to Him and get to know Him in a different way than we do in group settings.

Prayer is my constant communication with Him, my quality one on one time with Him. I love it!

I'm His Girl.

God is not a Genie

Naming and claiming something doesn't guarantee a favorable answer because prayer is not like a candy machine where I deposit the right kind of prayers and God gives me the answer I am looking for. Prayer is about a relationship. Don't get me wrong—prayer can change anything, and the Bible says that we should pray with all kinds of prayers and requests (Ephesians 6:18). But God knows the difference between being used and bossed around and a petition. If you aren't sure what your motive is, ask God to show you. Also remember this: any doctrine that promises a pain-free life if we only believe enough, do enough good works, or pray hard enough is setting us up for a nasty fall into a pit of believing God can't be trusted. In John 16:33 Jesus clearly reveals that to deny that trouble touches everyone is to deny the existence of sin when he says "In this world you will have trouble. But take heart! I have overcome the world!"

Are you struggling with trusting God because He hasn't answered your prayer the way you desire? Rather than believing that He isn't good or that He doesn't love you, choose to trust Him instead. You'll be glad you did.

"Though the fig tree does not bud and there are no grapes on the vines...yet I will exult in the LORD, I will rejoice in the God of my salvation..." (Habakkuk 3:17-18)

Prayer: Lord, I choose to trust You today even though You haven't said yes to all of my prayers. Forgive me when I have self-centered prayers. Help me to pray according to Your will and accept Your timing. I trust that my life, finances, family, job and everything is in Your capable hands. Help me to accept the things that I cannot change. Keep my focus intact. Create in me a clean heart and renew a right spirit in me as I walk this walk of faith with You! In Jesus' name, amen.

Christianity 101

Life is full of peaks and valleys, triumphs and tests. Faith is perfected & developed through life's fiery trials.

How do you prepare for the Test?
1. Go to Class
2. Listen to the professor
3. Study the notes

A student who skips class is ill-prepared for the test and it is pointless to ask the teacher for the answers when you didn't bother to show up, study or go to tutoring lessons. Especially when it was an open book exam!! You don't want to do the hard work but you want to reap the benefits of others' labor (prayer). If you cracked open the book the answers are readily available to you!

As a Christian we are not exempt from testing! As a matter of fact Jesus promised you will have MANY tests! He always gives preparation for each test that you will encounter but it's up to you, the student, to avail yourself of the tools made available in the Bible.

Leaders are instructed to teach and students are encouraged and expected to apply the teachings!

When it's time for the final exam you will either PASS OR FAIL – ain't no middle of the road!

Instead of enrolling in the class and paying the tuition we want to audit the class and still get the credit. Which means no commitment was required and no credit was gained.

If you don't pass the test, who failed you: the Teacher or yourself? You can't shortchange the process!

You're expected to come to class, attend lab (life class) & study on your own.

Do your best to present yourself to God as one approved, a worker who has no need to be ashamed, rightly handling the word of truth. But avoid irreverent babble, for it will lead people into more and more ungodliness. (2 Timothy 2:15-16)

Protect God's Gift

The anointing that we have is extremely precious and holy, and it is vital for every single one of us to know exactly how to protect the anointing that we have been given.

Unfortunately I have received numerous attacks for pressing into the supernatural and pressing to receive more of the anointing, more of Him. Not once have these attacks come from unbelievers but from precious peers in the body of Christ. I am learning to protect the gift that God has graciously given to me and to walk boldly in it. Just typing this makes me cringe because this could be perceived as arrogance. However, when you know that you have been anointed and appointed you can't walk in timidity. You've got to walk in the power of the One who entrusted you with this gift. I've decided to surround myself with people who will assist me in the process! The enemy doesn't fight fair! We are kingdom destroyers towards the enemy and KINGDOM conquerors for Jesus!!

The anointing is very very precious. The anointing is the real & tangible presence of God. The anointing is either present in someone's life or not. The anointing cannot be manufactured or fabricated!

But the anointing which ye have received of him abideth in you, and ye need not that any man teach you: but as the same anointing teacheth you of all things, and is truth, and is no lie, and even as it hath taught you, ye shall abide in him. (1 John 2:27)

I now know fully that God has a special anointing and calling on my life! I can't accept, allow or entertain living a mediocre Christian walk! I'm afraid BUT God told me while I was in Costa Rica to do it afraid! He has given me so much discernment that oftentimes I wish I could take back the request for it! He trusts me with it and I don't want to abuse it so I tread lightly with that anointing.

I say all of this because you have been chosen to walk with me in prayer. The enemy is attacking my body but I persevere. I need constant prayer. I refuse to give in to the enemy! I'm honored to be God's girl but it doesn't come without pain and suffering. But for the sake of the CROSS I will be obedient and walk in HIS anointing!

Humbly Submitted

Moving Forward

The simple reality for Paul was that, "though outwardly we are wasting away," his physical demise was not to be compared to the fact that "inwardly we are being renewed day by day" *(2 Corinthians 4:16).*

After sitting for awhile my bones ache! Realizing that I am aging! But that's not so much a bad thing. Viewed through the right lens, you could see yourself as day by day growing more wonderfully dependent on the grace and strength of God. My bent toward self-reliance and pride is being replaced with dependence and humility as I learn—perhaps out of necessity—to trust Him more and more.

I don't look forward to the aches and pains and the loss of what's left of my mind. The trials and burdens of life can make you feel ancient even at the tender age of 49! But with Paul's mindset, I can look forward to being more alive inside than ever before. And as far as aging goes, that's about as graceful as it gets!

Last night I got all dolled up and was shockingly dressed before my husband. I went downstairs in my "new" fur coat, stolen from my sister (she will never see this coat again, except on my back) and my daughter made me feel like I was about to be the belle of the ball! She said "Alright now Tina Turner!" While getting dressed I noticed my flaws: hair falling out, seeing the stress of life on my face, wanting a coke bottle shape (fail), the list goes on and on; so receiving that compliment from my baby girl made my night. My husband asking me to dance when he NEVER wants to made me feel young again so I cut a step and danced the night away! If only for one hour I felt no stress, I laughed hard and enjoyed a wonderful evening out.

The reality is I may be growing old in this body but each day I endeavor to live my life with purpose. There is honor involved with aging and growing old is normally accompanied by increase wisdom and experience.

Grey hair is a crown of splendor and is attained by a righteous life. (Proverbs 16:31)

Moving Forward/Challenge: March 1st I plan to get back on the bandwagon with eating better, working out, changing my mindset, speaking by faith and believing what I say! I was beginning to believe what I was seeing! Physically exhausted by life's stressors and wearing the weight of my & everyone else's burdens on my shoulders was bogging me down! I'm ready to spring forward! Speaking it before I see it is something my dear Sis Brenda spoke about at one of our church's Women Empowerment Engagements. I'm ready to live it out and become more positive NO MATTER WHAT!

Endure

The Bible repeatedly says that God has promised to meet your needs (Philippians 4:19). But the Bible also tells us that with every promise there is a condition. One of the conditions for this promise is that you have to trust him. The more you trust God, the more God is able to meet needs in your life. Faith is like a muscle: it develops by being used. The more you use your faith, the more it gets stretched. And the more it gets stretched, the more God is able to bless your life (1 Peter 1:7).

God doesn't test us because He doesn't know how strong we are. Instead, He tests us because we don't know how strong we are and we'll only realize it when times of testing come. The psalmist prayed, "Search me, O God, and know my heart; test me and know my anxious thoughts" (Psalm 139:23).

None of us likes to go through hard times (and God isn't necessarily causing them, even if He does allow them). But God can use them to show us our weaknesses. And when that happens, we need to ask God to help our faith grow. Testing should make us spiritually stronger and it will as we turn it over to God. The Bible says, "Consider it pure joy, my brothers, whenever you face trials … so that you may be mature and complete" (James 1:2, 4).

I'm in the midst of a huge test and I'm forced to trust God! Life is hard! Ministry is stressful! I want to see God's people blessed. I wish people could grasp on to the heart of God. It saddens me to the point of tears when people run from God during hardship; it breaks my heart when my husband and I are misread, misunderstood, lied on and disrespected. But the other side of this is that God rewards our faithfulness so even during the frustration there are blessings lurking. My faith is pointed towards the Father. My validation is not in man. I serve because I want to reflect God. He was mistreated, misunderstood and lied on BUT He endured. I can rejoice because I am like my daddy...an overcomer. So while I am in the midst of hurt and disappointment I can inwardly rejoice! I am a Kingdom minded girl! I may have my moments but I choose not to faint. We are victorious! We keep pressing, praying and praising because WE WIN!

Prayer: Father, search our hearts; forgive us for accepting Your blessings but running from You when tests and trials present themselves, even when you show us reminders that you are with us. Forgive us for being self-absorbed and acting like brats when we don't instantly receive what we want. Turn our hearts towards You. Help us to take our focus off material possessions and turn our hearts towards the things that please You! Father, help us forgive those who have falsely accused us and didn't understand us. Allow us to walk in love and embrace the difficult ones. Let us reflect You.

In Jesus' name, amen.

Christlike Love

Jesus tells us to love as he did: *"A new commandment I give to you, that you love one another: just as I have loved you, you also are to love one another." (John 13:34)*

I want to love like Jesus. I want to be generous, forgiving, and compassionate enough to love people unconditionally. No matter how hard I try I get so frustrated in trying to like people that are not friendly or who exhibit, for the lack of better words, unlikeable traits. One of the brothers said something in bible study years ago that echoed my sentiments: "I don't do stupid." I have a very low tolerance level for the childish stuff.

I can love, but I can't do it perfectly. Sometimes it's hard to make ourselves as vulnerable as Jesus did because we know we'll get hurt again. We love and at the same time we hold back.

Like branches on a vine, our Christian life is a growth process. Prayerfully we mature more every day. As we abide in Jesus, we learn to know him better and trust him more. Cautiously, we reach out to others and accept them for who they are, as we attempt to see them through the eyes of God. I am learning that the more I put my trust in God the greater my compassion is towards people. I am often diagnosing why this person did this or said that. Most times, through the lenses of offense, I realize that what people did or said can be portrayed as "stupid" or illogical but the underlying theme is that hurting people hurt people.

We live in such a fast-paced culture and the result is we want everything to come as a quick delivery. Love takes time to develop. Loving someone deeply requires taking the time to truly know them. It takes honesty, and vulnerability; it requires some risks and a tremendous amount of trust. Yet many people think they can just fast forward the process. Once that trust is broken it's like Groundhog Day! I am a living witness that it can be repaired ONLY if we love through God's eyes. It ain't easy!

Prayer: Father help me see people the way You do! Help me to walk in compassion and forgiveness. It's frustrating when people hurt or offend me to turn around and show them immediate grace as You do. I want to forgive quickly! Help me to love those who are different from me. In Jesus' name, amen.

Reflection: I fail plenty of times but God resets my course every time I ask. Real love takes work, has little applause, and presents lots of challenges. Love is a choice. Choose to love the unlikeable, it takes FAITH and it is possible!

The Language of Forgiveness

"While talking with him, Peter went inside and found a large gathering of people. He said to them: 'You are well aware that it is against our law for a Jew to associate with or visit a Gentile. But God has shown me that I should not call anyone impure or unclean.'" (Acts 10: 27-28)

Racism has always hurt my heart. The thought of one human being treating other human beings less than human because of their skin color makes my skin crawl. As a young girl visiting Mississippi for most of my childhood years I experienced it and watched it first hand when I saw others interact with my great grandmother and great grandfather. My heart quivered in grief and my eyes fill with tears when I feel the pain of injustice from the way the whites treated them and also me. I still experience the sting of racial sin. Thankfully, the unmerited suffering of racism is Christ's call to embrace His unmerited grace.

Peter confesses to a diverse group of Jews and Gentiles his culture's sin of racism. God showed Peter that no race is better than any other—to think, believe or act superior to another group of people is to commit the sin of racism. One race's claim of elitism over another grieves God! What one man may call unclean by their shameless ignorance is what the Lord calls clean. The birthplace of a person does not determine their value—being born in God's image defines a person's value.

It may come as a surprise to some that think I am a people person but really, really I am not. I love everyone but being comfortable around people who are not like me brings anxiety. I grew up primarily around blacks and Hispanics which at the time I thought were white. My world is so "black & white" in the literal sense of the word! So God has truly stretched me! I can embrace people who are not like me! Yesterday was another pivotal movement in my Christian walk. I was home visiting my dad and had the opportunity to go to his church (which I despise visiting) but it was Tuesday and my mama LOVES Tuesdays because that's the day their church serve the community who are less fortunate. Mom says they average over 300 weekly! They line up to get food! I was honored and privileged to meet and serve the people who didn't look or smell like me and it brought out so many emotions. We are so blessed, people! So blessed!

I choose to speak the language of forgiveness! If you have been treated harshly by other human beings because of your race remember Jesus' proclamation from the cross, *"Father, forgive them, for they do not know what they are doing"* (Luke 23:34)—I would encourage you lift up the cross of love and forgiveness.

I am celebrating Black History month by reading daily stories to my grandbaby about how we are overcomers and also reading scripture to her to show God's presence, even in past and present harshness against humanity.

Alcohol and the Church

This subject has been debatable for quite some time in the body of Christ. Having grown up so strict this was the ultimate no-no. I've witnessed many die because from the abuse of it. Homes destroyed because of alcoholism. More and more I am being made aware of saints partaking. I won't do it because my understanding of the scriptures pertaining to it leads me to believe that it could potentially ruin my testimony. So for me to drink it I would be sinning. I've heard some say they drink for medicinal purposes which I understand. Different cultures drink wine at dinner time; some drink because it's good for their digestive system; for others it helps them relax or sleep better. Is drinking alcohol wrong? I do not drink alcoholic beverages for one major reason: My conduct might cause someone else, who is weak, to stumble (Romans 14:14-21). While I know that I may fall short in areas and I can't live a perfect life I do strive to live a holy life.

Alcohol, consumed in small quantities, is neither harmful nor addictive from what I've heard. In fact, some doctors advocate drinking small amounts of red wine for health benefits, especially for the heart. Consumption of small quantities of alcohol is a matter of Christian freedom, I get that. Drunkenness and addiction however are sinful. Based on biblical concerns regarding alcohol and its effects – the ease of temptation to consume alcohol in excess or the possibility of causing offense and/or becoming a stumbling block to others – leads me to believe it is often best for a Christian to abstain from drinking alcohol. My body is the temple of the Holy Spirit. It is hard to think that we could pour liquor into the temple of God without defiling it. Liquor destroys blood vessels and brain cells. Long-term consumption of alcoholic can cause cirrhosis of the liver and it's hard for me to comprehend how we determine our threshold.

I looked online and found out that one ounce of liquor can begin to bring on intoxication; two or three ounces can make a person legally drunk. Half of all the traffic deaths in the United States are caused by people who have had at least one drink prior to driving. So to take our money, our lives, and our bodies – all of which belong to Jesus – and subject them to a state of intoxication can hardly be said to glorify the Lord or be an act of faith. Some would raise the issue of what Jesus did when He changed water into wine. When I researched it this is what I found: in ancient Israel there was almost no alcoholism, and there is little problem with it in Israel today. But in Jesus' day, wine was used at meals and in ceremonial functions or for special parties. As a national matter, wine was not a problem for them. Their wine was probably a low-alcohol-content grape derivative, and it was more of a refreshing beverage than it was an intoxicant. Jesus lived in a society in which alcoholism was not the problem that it is in our day. For Him, in the context of that culture, wine was all right. In today's society I don't believe the same context applies.

Here are some scriptures to consider:

1 Corinthians 6:19

1 Corinthians 10:31

Proverbs 20:1

Proverbs 23:31

Jesus said, *"I have come that they may have life, and that they may have it more abundantly"* (John 10:10). By using alcohol we participate in destroying not only our own life but often the lives of others. Even in moderation, alcohol use causes significant problems—physically, mentally, and spiritually. It's no wonder the Bible consistently warns against it. God says, in Isaiah 1:18 *"Come now and let us reason together."* With alcohol use we temporarily and permanently stupefy our reasoning powers. So, for a Christian, is alcohol drinkable, or unthinkable?

Burden Bearer

Just because someone may not seem depressed doesn't mean they aren't slowly dying inside. It is so easy to forget this, especially when we are all caught up in our own lives and problems and think that because someone looks like they are okay that they really ARE okay. I'm living proof that this is far from the truth. All that glitters ain't gold! Some can smile on the outside and be dying on the inside.

I repeat-**Do not ever assume that because someone SEEMS okay that they really ARE okay**. High-functioning depression is a big problem that's often invisible. Ask questions. Be proactive. Show you care. Speaking personally, I cannot even begin to tell you how much a few words of kindness can mean to someone who feels depressed. The closest I can describe is like someone turning the light on in a dark room. I'm not saying that you should think every "normal" person in your life has a mental illness, but please do your friend or family member a favor by checking in from time to time; it shows them that you do care. You never know – that person could be drowning with no idea how to ask for help.

I am yet bothered by the young man who recently took his young life here in Ohio. He seemed to have such a promising future and his family was so in shock by what transpired. I tend to attract people who will "dump" on me. I believe it's because I appear to care, which I do, but it's to my detriment. I was at a festive occasion on Friday evening and out of nowhere this lady (a stranger I might add) began to tell me her life story over a period of five minutes. I listened and offered a word of encouragement. She shared with me that she was a Social worker, and having worked as a liaison for a mental facility years ago I know first-hand the stress of that profession. After she shared her journey I asked a quick question: "So how do you take care of yourself after you've poured out so much." She said "I don't think about me I just tend to take care of others." This is not good! I'm learning to set boundaries and I believe this is something all of us should do before we become burned out! Before you know it you will find yourself spiraling into depression. The bible tells us to cast ALL our cares on Jesus! What does that actually mean? We are to commit EVERYTHING to Him: heavy trials, if we lose our friends & loved ones, or even health challenges. We can look to God for grace and strength and feel confident in knowing that he will enable us to sustain all that is laid upon us. The relief will be that God took the burden and bore it himself. Watch, the burdens will be lighter.

Galatians 6:2-5 says *"Carry each other's burdens, and in this way you will fulfill the law of Christ. If anyone thinks they are something when they are not, they deceive themselves. Each one should test their own actions. Then they can take pride in themselves alone, without comparing themselves to someone else, for each one should carry their own load."*

When we bear the burdens of our friends, we must keep in mind that we have to use discernment because even though we bear their burdens, we don't take them from them. Carry their burden BUT not their load! Bearing someone's burdens can be as small fixing a meal or something as POWERFUL as praying for that person. Prayer is so powerful and it is often the best thing we can do for someone who has a burden too heavy to bear alone.

It's a process. Start now by fully giving EVERYTHING over to God. You were not made to TAKE ON OTHERS' BURDENS. You may be strong but you ain't that strong! Give it to the one who WANTS to take it!

A Prayer for Peace of Mind:

God, I bless You for our lives. We give You praise for Your abundant mercy and grace we receive from You every morning! We thank You for Your faithfulness even though we are not that faithful to You. Lord we ask You to give us all-around peace in our mind, body, soul and spirit. We want You to heal and remove everything that is causing stress, grief, and sorrow in our lives. Please guide us through life and make our enemies be at peace with us. Let Your peace reign in our minds, family, at our place of work, businesses and everything we lay our hands on! God You came that we may have life abundantly.

Flaws and All

I am NOT your traditional Pastor's wife. Giving, nurturing, dreamer, misunderstood, unique, stylish, blunt, short, plump, caring, naive, smart, no filter, country, are just a few descriptions of your girl. This is how people view me. How God views us is what matters most.

God uses our flaws and our failings for incredible good - perhaps even greater good than had we been "perfect." When we stop comparing ourselves to others and put energy towards building the most important relationship we'll ever have, doors open to a life greater than we could have planned or achieved on our own!

It was laid heavily on my heart to have a conference in 2016. So many women compare themselves to others, allow society to define their worth, focus on the outer flaws and don't value why they were created or their purpose. I wanted a sacred day designed and fashioned particularly to the insecure and wounded sistas who needed a little encouragement and a boost to know that they can stay in the game a little longer and walk out the divine assignment given to them by God. You were handpicked, fashioned, loved, purposefully created, equipped and armed. Walk in authority with your head held high, shoulders squared and embrace the beautiful YOU! (Ephesians 1:4. Read the entire chapter...good stuff)

You are uniquely, fearfully and wonderfully made! Some fine tuning may be required. Get the manual out on how to repair the dysfunction. Your warranty has not expired! Walk in Authority and Victory!

Confession: Thank You, Father, for choosing me before I was ever born, before the foundation of the world. Thank You for setting me apart and making me blameless in your sight. You handpicked me because You loved me.

Take Me Away

I can remember when I was a kid growing up and would see those old Calgon bath product commercials that said, "*Take me away!*" Now that I'm a lot older, a full-time grandma, mentor and pastor's wife I've come better understand that phrase. Sometimes we need to be "*taken away*" from the daily grind. Our bodies are made to have a time of rest. If we don't rest from time to time we'll get worn down and perhaps damage our health. Resting rejuvenates us. This week I was under pastor's orders to rest!

"…and ye shall find rest unto your souls." (Matthew 11:29)

Rest is not just about getting enough sleep or relaxation for our bodies, although we need that. We also need rest for our minds and our souls. When we are worried or feel bad about doing something wrong, we can feel worn out. Jesus said, "Come to me, all you who are weary and burdened, and I will give you rest" (Matthew 11:28). By asking Him to take care of our worries and forgive our sins, we can have peace knowing that He loves us and will help us.

The heating pad has become a part of my body this week. It helps to ease the stress going down my back and neck. Having my children and husband dedicate pertinent time of prayer over me is helping to relieve the cares of life. My mama told me yesterday that people will stand over my casket and say she sure was a good woman and they will carry on with their lives. I am learning during this downtime that it's ok to say no; it's ok to rest, slow down and focus on healing. Having had so many health blows over the years, and even recently, I have to take time to heal. I am victorious and I am healed YET this body needs rest. I'm thankful to those who have covered me in prayer. I will be back in the game soon but having this week off is a great start.

Maybe it's time for you to slow down before your body slows you down! We can work ourselves to death – but it is God's purpose that will prevail. Do you find yourself in a crazy busy season of life? If so, take the time to rest in Jesus, allowing Him to prioritize your schedule.

Prayer: Dear God, Please help me (us) to slow down and rest in You. Give me (us) wisdom to discern what is important. In Jesus' Name, amen.

Words Aptly Spoken

Dr. Seuss is one of Braelyn's favorite books and yesterday it was mine! She wanted me to read to her over and over again. I believe we read a total of ten books but we had to read Dr. Seuss' Foot Book many times. After I finally told her "alllll done" she got off the sofa and began to march around saying left feet right feet repeatedly, to my amazement. I thought that was the cutest thing ever. Out of all the books we read the shortest one that was repetitive was her favorite one yesterday.

Less is often more. When it comes to being impactful with words, being long-winded is not necessarily valuable. But speaking the right words can be life changing. I am learning this principle when I speak and write. It's so challenging for me to condense my thoughts but I am a work in progress.

It's not how long we talk or how many eloquent words we use that matters. It is what we say that is so important. The words we use are like seeds. What we plant will grow.

I believe God gives us spiritual "radars" so we can assess a situation and speak the right word for that circumstance. In Colossians 4:6 Paul writes, "Let your conversation be gracious and effective so that you will have the right answer for everyone." We just need to check the "radar screen" before we speak. This is truly a convicting word for me especially since a whole lot of people ask me for my opinion. The other day my son skyped me and asked me how I liked his haircut and I said "It looks like your hairline is back to your earlobe. Why did you get it cut back so far?" Then my husband walked in while we were talking and he said "Boy your forehead looks like LeBron's." He laughed but I thought about it afterward and maybe I could've thought of something nicer to say like....you're handsome anyway! So I texted him later to apologize because I'm working on being tactful and he said "Mom I'm used to you, that didn't bother me."

Some people can't take my candor and I wished people wouldn't ask for my opinion BUT since they do I'm praying that God will help me to speak life. Now another child of mine got ALL of her hair cut a couple of days ago stating that she wanted a big chop. She came home and asked me how I liked it...let's just say I won't repeat what I told her! Then the next morning she combed it differently and asked me again how she looked. Again, I again won't share what I said but I ended it with saying "you are the one who has to look at it every day so that's all that matters." She smiled and said well at least that answer was better than yesterday's.

My son's girlfriend likes the "little boy" haircut on my son when I'd prefer it to be longer; my daughter likes the "natural" look on her and her baby but I prefer combed hair. It's preference: no right or wrong, just preference.

The right word – given at the right time and in the right way – can bring order in the midst of confusion, light on a very dark path, and wisdom to a questioning heart. Are we open to receive what we don't want to hear? From man? From God? When God doesn't answer the way we want or expect will we get offended? Laugh it off? Change or ponder?

My Prayer:
Father, I come today asking for Your forgiveness for the careless words I speak, however true they may be to me. Please teach me how to control my tongue and season them with salt. Please let people think twice about asking me my opinion because I'd much rather keep it to myself. Create in me a clean heart. Give me a holy desire to encourage and build others up with my words, especially with my family!

In Jesus' Name, amen.

True Repentance

True repentance always requires action. We must allow the sorrow we feel over our sin to lead us to reformed behavior and a **CHANGED** way of life. This is the fruit of genuine repentance. And here's the hardest part: you can never repent on behalf of someone else! You aren't responsible for others' sins and shortcomings. You can only take responsibility for your own actions and your own heart. So if you are tempted to either point out the failings of others, or to justify yourself in light of them, press pause and remember Jesus words, "unless *you* repent…"

Recently a family member sinned and their sin was a public sin. I was asked how I felt about their unfortunate failure and I looked perplexed because I was thinking long and hard before responding (which is growth for me because I would normally think and speak - hardly ever pondering the answer). I thought to myself well this is a ridiculous question; I didn't commit the sin so I don't live in condemnation over it. I pray for them and believe that God has forgiven them and I embrace the restoration process alongside of them.

"For the sorrow that is according to the will of God produces a repentance without regret, leading to salvation, but the sorrow of the world produces death." (2 Corinthians 7:10)

The Bible goes on in verse 11 of 2 Corinthians to show us in detail what godly sorrow looks like in the life of a believer:

For behold what earnestness this very thing, this godly sorrow, has produced in you: what vindication of yourselves, what indignation, what fear, what longing, what zeal, what avenging of wrong! In everything you demonstrated yourselves to be innocent in the matter.

We no longer desire to hide our sin but to get it washed clean. The temptation with sin is sometimes to hide it, to keep it from those around you and in some ways we think that we can keep it from God. However, this is of course foolish. Nothing can be kept from God and by hiding the sin we are simply continuing in it and prolonging our attack against God. The person who has experienced godly sorrow instead wants that sin cleansed from his/her life; they want it as far gone as the east is from the west and the only way to do that is to bring it before God and earnestly repent of it.

I had lunch with a dear friend yesterday and I mentioned to them that to continue in sin is like a dog returning to his vomit! The picture Solomon paints is both repulsive and sickening. To think that a dog, being sick with what he has eaten, vomits it up and would return afterward to lick it up is disgusting! However, that's the comparison Solomon gives to a fool who repeats his stupidity. The point being that **a dog is no more revolted by its own vomit than a fool by his own folly**; they both go back to that which is vile and disgusting. Why? Because the dog doesn't have any sense and neither does the fool. You may say that's insensitive and rude of you...um I'm just the messenger! Take it up with Jesus not with me. I'm a little frustrated with mature saints toying around with sin and abusing Grace.

Yesterday I received a call from someone I barely talk to. There was a sense of urgency in their voice so I listened attentively. After about 20 minutes into the call I challenged them. Here's the situation: this person is about to be sentenced to prison and wanted me to write them a sympathy letter to the judge as I'd done many years prior. I later found out from their attorney the lighter sentence was granted to them based on the letter I had written. Thank God for grace and mercy. Now fast forward, they've been "out of the joint "for approximately five years (or less) and they did well for almost 6 months. Less than one year after being released he allowed peer pressure to suck them back into the things of the world. He began to tell me he blamed his upbringing. However, when he insisted that he's learned their lesson and has been living right for the past three weeks that's when I interrupted.

Can you imagine what I said? Remember I am on a 30 day fast and one of the things I am working on is speaking life. With that being said I first offered a disclaimer and began to respond to that tomfoolery statement with asking them questions. Let's just say he admitted that although he should be held accountable for his sin he can no longer blame his past. There comes a time when TRUE REPENTANCE means to turn away! Nothing more, nothing less!

Moral of the story: true repentance brings about **_change_**!

Foundation

Everyone puts their hope and trust in something–and what we put our hope and trust in becomes our foundation for life. Some people build their lives on the foundation of money, believing that if they have more then life will be better and more secure. Some build their lives on possessions, trusting that more stuff means more happiness. Lots of people build their lives on popularity, thinking that if they can get more friends, they will never be lonely and life will be great.

Hope is a powerful feeling. It creates anticipation and affects not only how we think and feel, but how we act.

Hope deferred makes the heart sick, but a desire fulfilled is a tree of life." (Proverbs 13:12)

For as long as I can remember my nightly ritual in my marriage is when my husband and I get together at bedtime to talk, read a bible story & pray. What I love most about this time spent is a free back rub! Anyway, last night was a little different. Normally he leads but I wanted to talk, which is a rare. This is his time to pour into me, wash me with the word and again a free back rub! (Lol) I began to remind him of my goals I set for myself. Reminding him of the years I sacrificed my dreams so that I could help him and the kids accomplish their own. Now I'm feeling like life is now taking jabs and unexpected, sometimes redundant, punches that bring momentary frustrations. I walked him through 1984 when we first met in college, 1986 marriage, 1988 twins, 1990 grad school acceptance and another baby.....you get the picture. Every two years since we'd been together something major has happened but we conquered each one because of our foundation.

I'm grateful for the monuments we've built together and I attribute them to our strong foundation. However, I'm entering another season in my life – and am I wrong for wanting to add an accomplishment with my signature other than being a wife and mother?

I recall writing about Langston Hughes when I was in high school (which I'm shocked I remember):

What happens to a dream deferred?
Does it dry up
Like a raisin in the sun?
Or fester like a sore--
And then run?
Does it stink like rotten meat?
Or crust and sugar over--
like a syrupy sweet?
Maybe it just sags
like a heavy load.
Or does it explode?

Speech class, 1981, I choose this poem because I had dreams! Big ones! I remembered years prior to starting high school I sat on the hot porch talking to my great granddaddy in West Point, Mississippi. I was talking to him about a book Grandma Emma (his daughter) purchased for me to read on that long drive from Indiana., I read the poem to him and asked if he knew it to which he replied "yep show do." He proceeded to tell me that blacks (or colored people as he'd say) can't dream big because of the white man – they'd find a way to make you feel worse than a dog. He said "Yaw Ed Lee's gals, yaw good gals, you gone be like yo grandma C (her name was Cerula) and take good care of the kids and house." I couldn't wait for bed time so I could write in my diary. I believe that's the day I became a dreamer. As much as I loved and respected my great grandparents I wanted more out of life. Yes, I learned a lot spending countless summers down south, but I had dreams and I begin to tell about them in my speech. So fast forwarding to now some of these dreams have yet to be accomplished. The setbacks render frustrating moments and sometimes I have to fight through discouragement. I am reminding myself about my foundation - it is built to last because it is built on Christ, the solid rock on which I stand; all other ground is sinking sand! He will accomplish any and everything in His timing.

Dreamers keep dreaming!

Scars and Shame

Guilt says you've done something wrong and shame says you are something wrong. Don't believe that lie! God can and will bring peace to your past, purpose to your present and hope for your future!

The scars in my life are treasures. One in particular is childbirth. I thought that I would have natural childbirths however that was not so. My C-section for my twins (and Jazz) was scheduled so I asked Dr. Nirmala Pinnamaneni (best OBGYN ever) if I could be cut a certain way because I wanted to determine how my scar should look. She explained why I had to be cut the opposite way and at that time I was concerned about how the scar would look to my husband. She began to comfort me in saying that his love for me should far exceed the visual and the double blessings would erase the visual scars. She was absolutely right. I am reminded daily of the three blessings the scars produced. My most cherished gifts, my children.

Sometimes my most painful scars are the ones people cannot see which are the scars on my heart, the scars of disappointment or delayed dreams. Sometimes the scars are self-inflicted while other times they are caused others. The flip side is that wounds always heal. It takes time – and sometimes reconstruction and realignment – but it's an open invitation for God to intervene and perform the miraculous! The scars may be ugly to the natural eye but they are beautiful to God! The scars seen and unseen, ugly or painful as they may be can be redeemed and even used by God.

We tend to think of scars in negative terms. We are unhappy about how they look and they may be reminders of circumstances we would rather forget. But in our relationship with God those things are not necessarily negative. The enemy loves to trip us up, tempt us and sometimes make us fall. Rather than letting the pain of our scars defeat us and make us believe that we will never recover, God desires that we walk in a way that honors Him and make His name known through the painful present or past. God will make use of it to bring Himself glory. He can take our willingness to open up about it to encourage others. When I think of God's nail-scarred hands I know that scars can be beautiful. He turns our ugly scars into beautiful stars and places them on the mantel of His heart.

Prayer: God, sometimes the shame feels greater than the scars. But You said in Your word that You give beauty for ashes which lets me know that You are a comforter. Help us to look at our scars differently. Instead of seeing something unattractive or connected with suffering let us be reminded of all the lessons You have taught us and to be very thankful that we are not the same. Transform our thinking, help us to walk victoriously and help us readjust our thoughts and emotions. Let us be reminded of Your scars and remember that they represent Your presence in our lives and circumstances; because of them we are protected. Thank You for Your willingness to be scarred for me! Thank You for Your generous love. Help me to love like You, forgive like You and to run this race with grace. In Jesus' name, amen.

"You intended to harm me, but God intended it for good to accomplish what is now being done, the saving of many lives." (Genesis 50:20)

Security in Christ

Insecurity is an ugly thing. It can make you dislike people you don't even know and make you say and do stupid things. Everyone knows the saying that hurting people hurt people, sometimes intentionally and other times unintentionally. Many times we won't even know why we "hate on" folks and quite frankly I have little patience for these types of people. Let's face it we all have our insecurities; but we need to correct this behavior because it is toxic.

Feelings of insecurity drive us to believe we need to perform more. But performing more can lead to more insecurity. Being so performance-driven can lead to fragile egos, envy and jealousy.

We are told to let all thoughts of self become swallowed up in Jesus Christ.

Christ said, "Whoever desires to come after Me, let him deny himself, and take up his cross, and follow Me" (Mark 8:34). The word deny here literally translates to forget about yourself or lose sight of yourself. Basically stop being so "me" focused. PERIOD

Here is the key to becoming secure in who you were created to be: forget all about yourself and your agenda and become completely consumed with only one thing – GOD! Just as John the Baptist said, "He must increase, but I must decrease" (John 3:30).

Insecure people have challenges when they see people who know their callings and purpose and are confident in them. Those who struggle with insecurity are not great listeners and every topic is all about them. Become that person who yields to Christ and don't succumb to the enemy's sneaky schemes. When you do this your securities will come from a completely different source. Knowing your value and self-worth will come from knowing that you are redeemed and ever so loved by the King of all kings. I wish that people would turn their desires and focus to the things that matters the most.

There are women throughout the bible who truly glowed and each one had one common denominator: an emptying of self and the flesh. They were so caught up in the things of God that they gave no thought to their own lives. They did not seek to have eyes drawn to them. They sought to bring glory to Christ alone and as a result they were some of the most confident, poised and courageous women that have ever lived and accomplished amazing things for Jesus. And guess what? They did it without spending their time and energy focused on SELF.

Prayer: Lord let us realize that deep security comes from spending time in Your word and being in Your presence. It's knowing that you have accepted us, adopted us and we are guaranteed to have a future with You. Help us realize that we have nothing to prove to anyone and that there is no need to perform and no need to impress people because You have graciously accepted us. We are eternally secure in You because we "*have been crucified with Christ and I no longer live, but Christ lives in me*" (Galatians 2:20). Help us to live a life denying ourselves, taking up our crosses and following You as a full-fledged disciple. Help us to sucker punch the enemy in the eye by finding total security in You and not in stuff, people or our own self-worth. Lord, please let this prayer penetrate my heart and motivate me to make the necessary changes so that I can be effective to live out my purpose. In Jesus' name, amen.

LOVE LIVES

While he was in Bethany, reclining at the table in the home of Simon the Leper, a woman came with an alabaster jar of very expensive perfume, made of pure nard. She broke the jar and poured the perfume on his head.

Some of those present were saying indignantly to one another, "Why this waste of perfume? It could have been sold for more than a year's wages and the money given to the poor." And they rebuked her harshly.

"Leave her alone," said Jesus. "Why are you bothering her? She has done a beautiful thing to me. The poor you will always have with you, and you can help them any time you want. But you will not always have me. She did what she could. She poured perfume on my body beforehand to prepare for my burial. Truly I tell you, wherever the gospel is preached throughout the world, what she has done will also be told, in memory of her." (Mark 14:3-9)

Mary of Bethany did what she could. She gave from the context of who God had made her to be - and from what her relationship with Him was making her. She sat at Jesus' feet, opening her soul to His teaching, His wisdom, and His *love*. Because she took the time to take Him in, she "got" Him. Over the days, months, and perhaps years of their relationship, His investment reached to the core of her being and yielded a rich character from which she later anointed Him in a moment of His own great need. Spiritual intimacy had been formed and in return, it formed her. Such a powerful word picture for me!!!

Because she had received love, she gave it. She understood what, so far, the disciples had missed. In this act of worship, she lived love. Are you "living **love?**"

Mary approached Jesus with her gift of perfume and poured it out with confidence, her gesture expressing her love for Him and preparing His body for burial before His death, the broken flask foreshadowing the shards customarily left in the tomb after the body's anointing for burial.

Her gift touched Jesus in the moment, the fragrant oil running off His hair, down His temples and onto His neck and His chest, comforted him with love when it mattered most to Him.

I wonder whether later, Mary's gift gave again: as Jesus prayed at midnight tortured, by thoughts of what lay ahead and privately battling with His destiny; as He stood before the high priest, Pilate, Herod, and then back before Pilate, enduring their ridicule and accusations; as the thorny crown was smashed down on His head; as He bent His back under the lashes of the whips; as He struggled to carry a heavy cross through the streets of Jerusalem and up a dusty hill; as He was laid out on that cross and fixed to it by heavy iron nails through His hands and feet; and as He hung in crucifixion.

As His head fell to His chest, dipping under the weight of His suffering, did any fragrance still linger, mingled with the stench of blood, and bring back that tender moment?

Jesus gave Mary of Bethany access to Himself. Because she had fully received all He'd held out to her in His presence, His teaching and His very being, she had been forever changed. She acted from the reality of the relationship she shared with Him.

To Jesus, Mary gave a gift that kept on giving. She did what she could. She let Him **love** her.

He died so that I might live!

PERCEPTION

Sometimes we have faulty views and expectations we pick up by listening to bad teaching and bad advice, not to mention the cultural influence around us. Let's be clear: bad things do happen and they happen to good people. We will all go through trials, troubles, and tribulations. So what we have to do is figure out what to do when it happens.

What lesson do we learn from it and how do we grow better so we do not become bitter? We need to see His promises:

Read Psalm 46: 1

God does not look upon trouble as we do. Where we see stress He sees opportunities. When you are in the midst of trials it may seem like all hell has broken loose and the enemy has conquered. Don't believe that lie! God sees growth and betterment. God's purpose in times of crisis and trouble is to teach us, His precious children, life lessons. They are intended to educate us and build us up. And when we learn from them and ride out these storms of life, we will see the great promise fulfilled. We need to see the joy and opportunities through challenging times. Because we will learn that there is a sweet and wonderful joy we can have here too. We do not have to wait until heaven. We can learn to make our life joy filled by seizing the crisis and growing from it.

So when God tests you, or bad stuff happens, we need to see it as a time to learn and to trust Him by changing what is wrong with you while putting His promises in your heart. When it is over we can look back and see that our trials have been necessary. We are better because He is glorified!

All or most of these devotions are coming from my life experiences. I declare this year has brought unexpected changes and challenges in my home. Sunday I led prayer at my church for the first time and I shared with most who never knew I've had physical challenges because my praise is not predicated on how I feel. My praise is in knowing the outcome of the situation. I suffered some hard blows; however, each and every time God catches me, covers me and seals His promises with a kiss. I had a follow-up appointment with the doctor yesterday who once again wants to see me next week because my blood work is showing that my TSH levels are normal. Why are they skeptical of my healing? That's ok, I will go back for the last time because they ain't gonna keep poking on me and having my veins collapse just because they are skeptical! I am healed! Not a perception but a reality!

OVERFLOW

Do you ever feel like you're moving faster than the speed of light? More like moving at the "speed of life?" I'm there!

An old hymn describes grace as "amazing," and indeed it is! I may not be very graceful like two of my closest friends , but I consider myself to be full of grace which is not contingent on my physical attributes but it is contingent on my openness to the grace of God and my willingness to let it fill my life! ***OVERFLOW***

I am very intentional about never abusing grace. God's grace permeates every fiber of my being - so honored to be a recipient. The song, Amazing Grace, is sung by people all over the world but I wonder if they really understand its message. The idea of grace appeals to everyone and sometimes when it's given it can be abused and taken for granted.

In 2 Corinthians 9:8 we read: *And God is able to make all grace abound to you, so that in all things at all times, having all that you need, you will abound in every good work.* With God's abundant grace given to us Paul writes that we'll have all that we need, no matter what situation we're in, and we will be abounding in good works.

When God's grace fills us, then it must flow out to others. Be a dispenser of grace! Fulfill the good works that you were created to do. Ephesians 2:10 says *"We are God's workmanship, created in Christ Jesus to do good works, which God prepared in advance for us to do."*

Testimonial: "You can't beat God giving...no matter how you try, the more you give, the more He'll give to you. Just keep on giving because it's really true that you can't beat God giving....no matter how you try!" This is an old song that dropped into my spirit as I was writing. Late last night my husband and I were blessed for the 2nd time in our almost 30 years of marriage with an ALL expenses paid trip!!! I couldn't speak...I just cried! I am a huge giver, I have the gift to give, the anointing to give. I don't say that to brag at all, it's just the truth! God has taught me how to receive. I want others to experience that same adrenaline and the Godly principal associated with it. No matter how I give it ALWAYS.....DO YOU HEAR ME.....A.L.W.A.Y.S. comes back GREATER! Sow how you want to receive!

PRESCRIPTION

Have you ever been in a place where **everything** hits hard at once and the only prescription that can help comes from God?

Patient Name: Patrice L. (Chandler) Baker
Date: Henceforth, now and forevermore

Rx: Peace and Protection
Take as needed

Doctor Signature:
Almighty
Burden Bearer
Comforter
Deliverer
Emmanuel
Friend
Giver of every good and perfect gift
Healer
I Am
Judge
King of kings
Lord of lords
Master
Name above all names
Overseer
Prince of Peace
Quieter of storms
Resurrection and the Life
Savior
Truth
Upholder
Victor over death, hell, and the grave
Word made flesh
eXample
Yoke-mate
Zealously in love with Patrice & her seed

This is one time it is legal for me to share my prescription! Take as needed!

PERSECUTION

Are you prepared to handle the persecution that comes with your blessing or with moving to the next dimension? Just as God promised to bless you He has also promised that you will have trouble. Many of us are ready for our dreams to come true. But are you prepared? The reward doesn't come without persecution (Mark 10:30) but there is an end in sight. When we are in the midst of pain our vision is obscured and it's difficult to see that there is a blessing in persecution. We begin to doubt the saying that trouble don't last always and we begin to think "yeah right!" We get so stuck in the moment and in the pain that we fail to realize WHAT this moment was meant to teach us! We are disappointed and afraid to move forward because we become comfortable in our pain and begin to wear it like a pair of worn out but comfortable shoes. I wish that life were easy but God wants you to remind you of the truth about you and your identity.

There are people who will take comfort in your pain because of their insecurities but don't allow them to distract you; just let your haters to become your audience. Have you ever been ready to put on your boxing gloves but instead you saw Jesus go before you in a situation? Our own insecurities make us afraid. Being uncomfortable makes us afraid. Walk into persecution with your head held high because on the other side of affliction is your victory! The glory on the other side will far outweigh the pain of this moment! So when it's your time to be like Christ will you stand tall or will you shrink back? Exposure is everything. Once you've been exposed you can't go back to pretending that you didn't know. If I'm so afraid of what lies ahead until it makes me shrink then I run the risk of staying stagnate; even though the uncertainty of what's next makes me want to say "good grief I just can't take no more!" The blessed hope is that there is DESTINY designed, fashioned and available just for you if you PUSH through. Hold on to your faith, though it may be small as a mustard seed, despite never ending, constant blows. We have to believe that what lies ahead is far greater than anything we've left behind. God sees the tears and the disappointment but we can stand the breaking that comes with persecution. Persecution is custom-made for you! It is inevitably connected to your destiny. It is unique to your identity, designed for your shoulders – not your mama's or your spouse's or friends, but just for you. God knows what you can bear. Have faith that the God who allowed it will bring you out of it victoriously!

Father, I thank You that this trial won't cause my heart to become hardened or consumed with the trouble that's been assigned to my name. I am afraid but also amazed at where you are taking me. Prepare me for the battle. Help me not to grow weary when my heart seems to skip a beat due to the pressure of pain. Hold me in Your arms when I feel like I am so alone. Help me as I break into the next level of transition so that I never lose the hope and faith that You are forever present. Help me to master this level of persecution so that I am ready for the next dart that the enemy has prepared for me. Let me not look at people or circumstances surrounding the pain as something I can't conquer. Instead, help me to believe that I was chosen for this trial so I may come out shining bright and brilliant and so that you may obtain all the glory. Let me not become bitter but help me get better. I'm entering a new level of grace through my pain. I am empowered and equipped to be and do all that You created me to be. I am safe in Your arms and thankful that You chose me for this persecution.

Movin' on Up

"Even though things still seem strange, unpredictable, and unsettled, you can rest assured that I know every detail of your circumstances. I hold your times and seasons in My hand," says the Lord, "and I will establish, settle, and strengthen you in the purposes of My will. All you have to do is trust Me and obey My leading. Doubt, frustration, and double-mindedness will get you nowhere. Make a quality decision now to stand in faith that I will lead the way and bring you through this difficult time into triumph. "

The Lord has something in mind and that is to establish us on a new spiritual level and settle us in a new spiritual land. Yes, uncertainty about tomorrow is scary when seen through my horrible vision! I have to constantly step outside of my feelings and go beyond what my natural eyes can see and trust the one who has vision and purpose for my life. It's so easy to "speak it" but it's miraculous when you actually believe it. Why do we doubt what God has for us? Our faith has to be ignited. It's time to relinquish what we can see and begin to visualize the blessed hope. I had breakfast with one of God's sweetest women yesterday. Her faith sparked something in me, almost childlike. She said she expects to win and the more we conversed she began to explain her expectancy over every area of her life. She said it so confidently and I saw in her posture that she meant what she was saying! I listened to what she said – and the passion with which she said it – and meditated on it for hours after we departed. These are the type of people I choose to converse with! I no longer have time to embrace or tolerate people in my inner circle who expect mediocrity! I desire increase in every area of my life!

I know that a transition is right upon me! I asked God what does this look like? This is what I feel His reply was:

1. Don't let fear drive you

2. Don't grumble or test (question) Me

3. Don't allow unbelief rule

4. Don't rebel (disobey His Word)

5. DO understand that you are appointed and anointed and I will lead you like a blind person every step of the way; you will know what to do and how to do it at the appointed time.

I am calling you forth to a new level of faith and a brand new experience! If you could but see My purposes that have been established for the end of the age you would rejoice! All of your troubles, all of your heartache, all of your worry, all of your anxiety, all of your trials, would diminish in the power of the anointing that I shall place upon you!

Put Your Past Behind You

"Make your past a place of <u>reference</u> not <u>residence</u>."

Let's learn from the past, but not dwell on it. Sometimes we can get stuck there. My husband sometimes shares stories with the congregation about some of his high school buddies who are stuck in 1984. Stuck in the pain, traditions, style and thinking that hasn't progressed beyond teenage years. What a sad state of affair!

I press toward the mark for the prize of the high calling of God in Christ Jesus. (Philippians 3:14)

We are constantly to be moving forward, growing and doing all we can to get the message of God's love to others. We must make sure that we are living a life that reflects Christ's nature in order to attract others to Him. Our past mistakes are not wasted mishaps. Use them as a testimony to help others overcome. Some of our past carries shame but choose not to allow the enemy to trick you into living in shame. Flip the script on him and rejoice in knowing that you are free from the past and with that no condemnation will dominate you any longer!

Your beginnings will seem humble, so prosperous will your future be. (Job 8:7)

Your present circumstances should not define your future. Likewise, your past circumstances should not determine your future. God has given you the ability to move forward and make progress in your life. Do not incarcerate or imprison yourself mentally! The human spirit, when aligned with God's Holy Spirit, has the ability to rise above any limitations. Our wonderful imaginations given to us by God allow us to see what is unseen. Incredibly, we are all capable of turning what we imagine into reality.

We cannot change our past. We cannot change the fact that people will act a certain way. The only thing we can do is adjust our mindset and keep moving towards our destiny. The truth of the matter is that life is going to happen – sometimes for the better and sometimes for the worse. The one true thing that you will always have 100% control over is your response to these events. I've heard it said that it is very rare or almost impossible that an event can be negative from all points of view. Life is like riding a bike: you must keep your balance and keep it moving or you will fall! Falling doesn't mean failing, you just lick your scars, patch yourself up and get back on your grind! Finish well and finish strong! It is from failure that growth comes, provided you can recognize it, admit it, learn from it, rise above it, and then try again.
You've been served notice...you are an overcomer!

Lights, Camera, Action

I've done TV commercials off and on for the past 20 plus years. When I would practice my lines at home I was fine but the moment the spotlight was on I felt a little uncertain, especially if the director was fussy or on edge. One particular time I yelled "cut!" Boy that made the director angry and they called my agent in a fury. I told them repeatedly that I was uncomfortable with my onset husband placing his hands around my waist yet he seemed to forget each time we did a retake. When the camera was off and we were rehearsing our lines we did so well; yet, knowing that we'd be critiqued or in the spotlight is when the nerves would come, causing cause us to mess up. However, we eventually we got it right and were able to finish the commercial.

This scenario makes me wonder: what do you do when no one's looking? What happens when you know you won't get caught? What do you do when you don't see the camera? If you're insensitive to just doing what's right when the camera's rolling will you also become insensitive to the things of God? Think about the times you missed a church service here and a church service there. Soon enough one service became three services and eventually a month has gone by. Slowly you become comfortable with fewer restraints – doing things your way – and the conviction of Holy Spirit becomes faint. So many people of God believe that grace is a pass to do as they desire at the expense of righteousness. Jesus did not come to do away with the law but to perfect it. We may not have the same penalties since we are under grace, but we forfeit the benefits of grace and righteousness by choosing to do our own thing.

Don't frustrate the grace of God. Our Father is counting on us. Let's commit to keeping our hearts pliable to the conviction of Holy Spirit and adhere to doing what's right, regardless of whether we see the cameras.

Rest Renewed

When you are exhausted and burned out from the cares of life you can begin to act out of your emotions. Just a few days ago that happened to me. I received some disturbing news that a close friend of mine was hurt by someone's insensitive words and immaturity and I became very angry! They remained calm but I was so upset to see them so down because of it. I told my husband that I wanted to punch their accuser and then step on their pinky toe! He was in shock because I am not the violent type! My first reaction is never one of violence. I was just like a tired baby who does all manner of silly stuff – I was; tired, worn out, beat down, stretched and stressed! Thank God for my adult children who were deeply concerned about me and generously blessed me with a few days away in the sun and tranquility. This has been an amazing three-day getaway! I feel like I can conquer the world now!

Mental stress that goes on too long can lead to exhaustion and eventually can cause a breakdown. The body cannot maintain ongoing stress for a long period of time. When I'm stressed I've noticed that my heart works harder and my back bears the pain caused by my stress. At some point the body will not keep operating properly and during the exhaustion phase health problems and even death may occur. When my doctor shared this information with me I knew immediately I had to find ways to eliminate and/or learn how to deal with stress. This is a continual process but I am fighting hard to set boundaries. I am a planner so in this next phase of my life I'm learning how to limit my commitments and reach out for help because I have been blessed with a wonderful group of ladies who continually offer to assist me. Moving forward my theme will be 1 Peter 5:7. I, Patrice, will take ALL of my worries to you Daddy because You are better equipped and beyond capable of dealing with them. I will no longer act like I'm Jesus Jr.! While I want to mirror You I am not You! You are good at working solo so I'm getting back in my lane! I get it!!